NUTRITIVE COOKING FOR CHILDREN

Dr Shaila Santhanam, a garduate in medicine from Pune University, did her internship in AIIMS, New Delhi. Soon after she got an opportunity to work as a consulting doctor with a leading slimming and health-care company with centres all over India. This was a turning point in her life as she dealt with many adults suffering from various forms of illnesses resulting from unhealthy eating patterns like obesity.

Shaila has also done extensive research in the field of Ayurveda and allied sciences to broaden her view and understanding of nutrition. About this time, she began work on a recipe book aimed at providing children with holistic nutrition. The idea was also to make nutrition an intrinsic part of the upbringing of a child as well as to provide easy and delicious options for parents to choose from. A year later, *Nutritive Cooking for Children* was ready!

OTHER TITLES

1000 Great Indian Recipes
Aphrodisiac Cuisine
Art of Indian Cuisine
Buddhist Peace Recipes
Bukhara
Food Path: Cuisine Along the Grand Trunk Road from Kabul to Kolkata
Hindu Soul Recipes
Indian Barbecue
Indian Flavours
Indian Recipes Under 30 minutes
Indian Spa Cuisine
Moti Mahal's Tandoori Trail
Street Foods of Indian
The Gourmet Indian Cookbook
The Indian Vegetarian Cookbook
The Landour Cookbook

CHEFS' SPECIAL SERIES

Bengali Kitchen
Delhi Kitchen
Dum Cuisine
Favourite Indian Desserts
Goan Kitchen
Gujarati Kitchen
Iyer Kitchen
Kerala Kitchen
Marwari Kitchen
Parsi Kitchen
Punjabi Kitchen
Rajasthani Kitchen
South Indian Vegetarian Kitchen
Tandoori Cuisine

FORTHCOMING TITLES

Awadhi Kitchen
Gourmet Journeys Through India
Indian Fast Food
Kashmiri Cuisine Made Easy
Moti Mahal's Tandoori Trail: The Butter Chicken Cookbook
Pure and Simple Vegetarian Cookbook
The Emperor's Table: The Art of Mughal Cuisine
The IT Cookbook

NUTRITIVE COOKING FOR CHILDREN

Dr Shaila Santhanam

Louts Collection

This edition published in 2006
Second impression, 2008
The Lotus Collection
An imprint of Roli Books Pvt. Ltd.
M-75, G.K. II Market, New Delhi 110 048
Phones: ++91 (011) 2921 2271, 2921 2782
2921 0886, Fax: ++91 (011) 2921 7185
E-mail: info@rolibooks.com; Website: rolibooks.com

Also at
Bangalore, Chennai, Jaipur,
Kolkata, Mumbai and Varanasi

Editor: Neeta Dutta
Cover Design: Supriya Saran
Layout design: Naresh Mondal

ISBN: 978-81-7436-416-6

s Light by Roli Books Pvt Ltd.
Printed in Anubha printers Noida

Contents

Foreword 6
Nutritional Reference 8
Height-Weight Charts 9
Articles 11
Food Guide Pyramid 17
Childhood Obesity 23
Table Manners 33
EQ 37
The Mind of the Adolescent Eater 41
Home Cooking Safety Tips 43

DRINKS AND BEVERAGES 49
SNACKS AND STARTERS 63
MAIN COURSE 93
SWEETS AND DESSERTS 117

Glossary of Cooking Terms 126
Index 128

Foreword

In my experience both as a doctor and as a keen observer of modern living, I have seen far too many people live their lives in oblivion of what they eat and what impact it has on their lives. To me, what is saddening still, is the fact that their children are raised in such environments. It is with a view to enlighten parents about the nutritional requirements for their children that the idea of this book came about.

Nutrition as a subject is not one that is alien to me. The knowledge I gained while studying to be a doctor was vast and comprehensive. Medicine not only taught me the basics of nutrition, it provided me with deep insights into the workings of our body and gave me a holistic picture of nutrition from the inside out. My endeavor in this book is not to propound my theories, but to present to the reader a collection of credible information from institutions of international repute, that would enable parents to make informed decisions about the right diet for their children.

This book is not about a singular diet regime, on the contrary, it is sensitive to the socio-cultural diversity of civilization and is, in that sense, a democratic book, one of options instead of opinions and limitations. A wholesome and nutritious diet only requires two things: minor alterations in your current diet to ensure everything consumed is within the adequate range and, if required, a few additions to ensure you get all the nutrients that your body needs.

Nutrition is a science. It is a qualitative and quantitative science. However, while researching for this book, one thing became quite evident to me. Modern research in the field of nutritional sciences is almost in its infancy when compared to institutions like Ayurveda. Also, modern nutritional science seems to change its opinion far too frequently. Therefore, in this book, I have tried to fuse information and perspectives from both the old and the new.

I hope that *Nutritive Cooking for Children* goes a long way in providing you with a solid foundation of understanding nutrition and the nutritional requirements of your children.

Nutritional Reference

Serving Sizes

Item	Serving Size
Grains	
Breads	One slice of bread
Rice	1/2 cup of cooked rice
Pasta	1/2 cup of cooked pasta
Cereal	1/2 cup of cooked cereal
Vegetables	
Raw Vegetables	1/2 cup
Cooked Vegetables	1/2 cup
Leafy Vegetables	1 cup
Fruits	
Apple	1 medium-sized apple or 1/2 cup chopped
Banana	1 banana or 1/2 cup chopped
Orange	1 medium-sized orange
Pear	1 pear or 1/2 cup chopped
Canned Fruit	1/2 cup
Fruit Juice	3/4 cup
Dairy	
Milk	1 cup
Yoghurt	1 cup
Cheese	45-60 gm
Protein	
Meat/Poultry/Fish	60-90 gm
Beans	1-1 1/2 cups cooked beans
Eggs	2 eggs
Peanut Butter	2 tbsp

Height-Weight Charts

For Boys

Age	Weight (kg)	Height (cm)
Birth	3.3	50.5
3 months	6.0	61.1
6 months	7.8	67.8
9 months	9.2	72.3
1 year	10.2	76.1
2 years	12.3	85.6
3 years	14.6	94.9
4 years	16.7	102.9
5 years	18.7	109.9
6 years	20.7	116.1
7 years	22.9	121.7
8 years	25.3	127.0
9 years	28.1	132.2
10 years	31.4	137.5
11 years	32.2	140.0
12 years	37.0	147.0
13 years	40.9	153.0
14 years	47.0	160.0
15 years	52.6	166.0
16 years	58.0	171.0
17 years	62.7	175.0
18 years	65.0	177.0

For Girls		
Age	Weight (kg)	Height (cm)
Birth	3.2	49.9
3 months	5.4	60.2
6 months	7.2	66.6
9 months	8.6	71.1
1 year	9.5	75.0
2 years	11.8	84.5
3 years	14.1	93.9
4 years	16.0	101.6
5 years	17.7	108.4
6 years	19.5	114.6
7 years	21.8	120.6
8 years	24.8	126.4
9 years	28.5	132.2
10 years	32.5	138.3
11 years	33.7	142.0
12 years	38.7	148.0
13 years	44.0	150.0
14 years	48.0	155.0
15 years	51.5	161.0
16 years	53.0	162.0
17 years	54.0	163.0
18 years	54.4	164.0

Articles

The who's who of the nutritional world

Nutrition is a qualitative and a quantitative world. It groups foodstuffs according to their nutritional break-up and then quantifies how much of what one should be consuming. Without knowing the basic structures that make up this world, it would prove hard to get around. There are vitamins, proteins, carbohydrates, fats, minerals, and fibre, and to each there are types and quantities of each type. Let us begin this with an introduction to vitamins.

Vitamins are responsible for all round growth of a human being. There are 10 vitamins in the nutrition world.

- Vitamin A (Retinol)
- Vitamin B_1 (Thiamin)
- Vitamin B_2 (Riboflavin)
- Vitamin B_3 (Niacin)

- Vitamin B_6
- Vitamin B_{12}
- Vitamin C (Ascorbic Acid)
- Vitamin D
- Vitamin E
- Vitamin K
- Vitamin B_5 (Pantothenic Acid)

Each of these vitamins play a vital role in the different aspects of a child's life. Vitamins have unique chemical attributes and sources as well. For example, vitamin C is a water-soluble vitamin that is essential in the formation of collagen, a chemical that keeps you from bruising too easily and is found in abundance in orange juice. On the other hand, vitamin A is a fat-soluble vitamin that is essential for eyesight and growth among many other things and is found in carrot.

The table below enlists vitamins, their functions, and their sources:

Vitamins

Name	Function	Source
Vitamin A	Essential for eyesight, growth, cell division, bone and teeth development, reproduction, maintenance of the immune system, formation of hair, skin and mucous membranes	Vegetarian: carrot, dark green leafy vegetables like spinach, oranges, eggs Non-vegetarian: liver and fish

Name	Function	Source
Vitamin B_1	Essential for releasing the energy stored in carbohydrates and the creation of a chemical used by the nervous system	Vegetarian: rice bran, soya, flour, and wheat germ Non-vegetarian: pork
Vitamin B_2	Aiding the release of energy stored in carbohydrates, proteins and fats, maintains the mucous membranes, promotes growth, and maintains healthy skin and eyes	Vegetarian: milk and milk products, whole grains and enriched cereals, broccoli, asparagus, and spinach Non-vegetarian: meat, poultry, and fish
Vitamin B_3	Primarily involved with the production of energy inside cells. Also helps in the maintenance of the digestive and nervous system	Vegetarian: grains, enriched cereals, and foodstuffs high on protein
Vitamin B_6	Responsible for formation of red blood cells, assists in the formation of genetic material, aids the functioning of the nervous system and helps	Vegetarian: whole-grain breads, spinach, and bananas Non-vegetarian:

Name	Function	Source
	convert tryptophan, a substance found in high protein foodstuffs, to Vitamin B_3	liver, meat, and poultry
Vitamin B_{12}	Aids in the formation of red blood cells, helps with the nervous system, and assists with the formation of genetic material	Vegetarian: yeast, milk and milk products Non-vegetarian: liver, meat, fish, eggs, and oysters
Vitamin C	Essential for formation of collagen in the skin. It also helps maintain blood vessels, bones and teeth	Vegetarian: orange juice, citrus fruits, tomatoes, strawberries, green chillies, potatoes
*Vitamin D	Essential for the absorption and use of calcium and phosphorous by the body. Also responsible for the maintenance of bones and teeth	Vegetarian: fortified milk Non-vegetarian: fatty fish like salmon
Vitamin E	Aids in the formation of red blood cells and muscles. It protects vitamin A and essential lipids from oxidation	Vegetarian: vegetable oils, whole grain cereals and breads, green leafy vegetables

Name	Function	Source
Vitamin K	Essential for the formation of prothombin that enables clotting of blood, plays a vital role in maintaining proteins, plasma, the kidneys, and the skeletal system	Vegetarian: green leafy vegetables, cabbage and cereals
Vitamin B_5	Plays a vital role in the creation of hormones that fight allergies and assist metabolism. Beneficial also in the maintenance of healthy skin, muscle and nerves.	Vegetarian: Fresh green vegetables, legumes, nuts and whole wheat.
* Vitamin D is actually produced by the body (technically speaking, this makes it a hormone) through exposure to sunlight. Roughly 15-20 minutes of sunlight is adequate to meet your vitamin D requirements.		

Phytochemicals

These are naturally occurring substances found in foodstuffs. Phytochemicals are found in colourful vegetables, legumes, herbs, and spices. They are believed to decrease your chances of developing cancer and heart disease. Some of these phytochemicals can block carcinogens before they make a cell cancerous, while others slow down the growth of cancerous cells.

Antioxidant

These are a group of compounds, namely, vitamin C, vitamin E, and beta-carotene that are found in common foodstuffs. These antioxidant defend your cells against damage caused by unstable oxygen compound called free radicals. They also help in reducing the risk of cancer, cataracts, and heart disease amongst other diseases. Incredibly they also slow down the ageing process.

Food Guide Pyramid

What should a child be eating to fulfil her daily nutritional needs? How well is a child doing in her current diet? What more should a child be eating? It is with these questions in mind that the USDA (United States Department of Agriculture) came up with a pyramidal structure called the Food Guide Pyramid or the FGP.

The structure divides all foods into six categories:

- Fats, Oils and Sweets
- Milk Products Group
- Meat and Bean Group
- Vegetable Group
- Fruit Group
- Grain Products Group

Examples of foodstuffs within these groups are provided in the table below.

Fats, Oils and Sweets	Ghee, Chocolates, Cooking oils, etc.
Milk Products Group	Yoghurt, Milk, Cheese, Butter, Paneer
Meat and Beans Group	Meat, Chicken, Fish, Pork, Beans
Vegetable Group	Potatoes, Cauliflower, Spinach
Fruit Group	Oranges, Apples, Grapes, Bananas
Grain Products Group	Rice, Wheat, Pulses, Barley, Maize

The basic principle behind the pyramidal structure is to quantify how much of what one should eat in order to derive adequate nutrition from one's diet. To follow this diet regime is to ensure that one eats at least the minimum prescribed amount from each strata a day, as shown in the diagram on the facing page.

As you can see from the diagram, the fats, oils and sweets group occupy the topmost strata of the structure. The FGP recommends minimum consumption of all items that fall in this category. The Milk Products Group and the Meat and Beans Group follow this group. 2-3 servings of each of the Milk Products Group and 150-180 gm of the Meat and Beans Group are recommended by the FGP. Below these strata, you will find the Vegetable Group and the Fruit Group. The FGP recommends

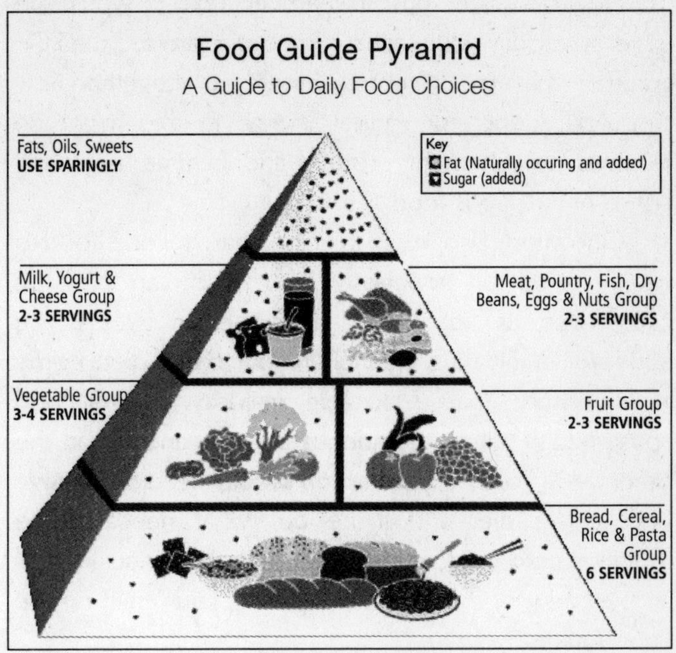

consumption of 3-4 servings from the Vegetable Group and 2-3 servings from the Fruit Group. At the very bottom of the pyramid one would find the Grain Products Group and the FGP recommends consumption of 6 servings from this group.

Therefore, if you can ensure that your child's diet is within at least the minimum prescribed serving quantity of each group, then you could be certain that your child is eating a nutritious diet and she is deriving adequate nutrition from it.

However, one must remember that it would be easier to modify your child's current diet around the FGP gradually than to attempt to initiate an altogether new diet. Any sudden or radical change in diet might be received by vehement protests and, in time, a general dislike of nutritious food.

One must also keep in mind that no one food is wholly good or hopelessly bad. Food can only be categorized as adequate, inadequate or excess. The endeavor in initiating the FGP in your child's diet regime is to ensure that a suitable majority of the food consumed is within the adequate range, and not in the other two. So, as a parent you would need to analyze your child's diet and figure out what needs to be modified before adding new items on the menu. Here is an overview of the process in getting your child on the Food Guide Pyramid.

FGP installation overview

Active or passive participation on the part of your child is a decision you will need to take yourself, based on her intelligence and sensibilities.

Details of this process are provided below:

- List current diet
  a. List all the foodstuffs consumed in a day
  b. Approximate respective serving sizes consumed

- Analyze current diet
    a. Compare consumption in current diet with recommendations of the FGP
    b. Slot foodstuffs into three slots: adequate, inadequate and excess
    c. Adjust the values in the three slots to within the adequate range and make a note of the remainders adding the appropriate + or - sign
    d. Ensure all categories within the FGP are present in the list. If not, be sure to make a note of the categories

- Modify diet
    a. If there are any categories in the FGP that are absent in the consumption list, add foodstuffs from the category, that you think your child may like to add to the consumption list
    b. If there are any remainders in the negative, that is, in the inadequate slot, add alternative foodstuffs to make up for the deficit
    c. Similarly think of appropriate alternatives for foodstuffs that are in excess

Now you have a wholesome diet on paper and you have a fair idea of what your child should be consuming in a day. All that is left is to add further variety to the food and get the child to actually start consuming what is on paper. Since your child will find it hard to eat the same diet everyday it is important to provide her with some variety. Therefore, in order to make things a little more interesting for your child, you would need to look at attractive, nutritious alternatives that would allow a slow but sure change in your child's eating patterns. The recipes provided later in this book will prove very handy in finding new or alternative meals for your child.

When attempting to install a wholesome and nutritious diet pattern in your child's life, try not to look for instant results. Slow and gradual persuasion and casually guiding your child towards nutritious eating is the best way to get her going.

Childhood Obesity

Obesity is a large subject. Euphemistic perhaps, but in most cases it plays havoc with every single sphere of modern living. From obvious physical ramifications to deep-seeded complexities that haunt the mind throughout one's life, obesity in your child's life could be just a passing phase or a nightmare that could potentially last a lifetime.

However, well before one starts sounding alarm bells, one needs to ascertain whether the obesity is a serious condition or a temporary state. Obesity could be due to a number of reasons. It could be due to an eating disorder, a metabolic disorder, or a genetic condition.

Eating disorder:

Symptoms: Irregular eating patterns, unhealthy eating habits

Metabolic disorder:

Symptoms: Learning disorders, attention disorders, muscle wasting, stunted growth, Cushing's syndrome, hyper/hypothyroidism

Genetic disorder:

Symptom: Will be visible from birth

How do you know that your child suffers from an eating disorder?

Identifying eating disorders in your child

These are the various traits one should look out for:

- If the food disappears from the fridge suddenly
- If the child raids the fridge at odd hours
- Prefers to eat alone
- Seems to put on weight even though the appetite is normal
- Eating small portions
- General refusal of food
- Intense fear of being fat
- Non-stop exercising
- Becoming secret eaters
- Disappearance after eating, often to the bathroom

- Great fluctuations in weight
- Large amounts of food disappearing quickly

Now if the above symptoms exist what should the plan of action be?

Here are some other tips to help you and your obese child:

Be a positive role model. 'Parents play a vital role in the development of their children,' says Dr. Philip Fischer, M.D., a pediatrician at Mayo Clinic, Rochester, Minnesota. 'Take notice of lifestyle habits that can contribute to overeating and inactivity in your children, then set a good example.'

You can make subtle lifestyle changes to help your kids eat healthier. Limit portion sizes. Make an effort to cook with less fat, for example; bake foods instead of frying them. Do not order French fries if you do not want your kids eating them. Do not buy chocolate cookies if you don't want your kids sneaking a few from the cookie jar. Likewise, your child will be more willing to snack on fruits and vegetables after seeing you doing the same.

Get active. Try to plan activities that get the whole family moving, such as playing football, cricket, etc. Make an after-dinner walk a regular part of your family's evening. Remember that exercise does not have to be hard work. Gardening, running through the sprinkler, bathing your pet under supervision, dusting the house, etc. are all good options.

Make eating an activity in itself. 'Eating is a significant event, and it should be enjoyable,' says Dr. Fischer. 'Kids, especially overweight ones, should not eat while watching television, riding in a car or walking through the kitchen. They should sit down just to eat, enjoy the meal and then get up and do something else fun.'

A good way to accomplish this goal: reinvigorate the family dinner. Setting aside time to eat together at the table will help you monitor your child's food intake and will give you some quality time together. Get the kids involved in the menu choices, meal preparations, and in the cleaning up, too.

Instead of rewarding your children with snacks, teach them to use food for energy. Rather than treating your child to an ice-cream cone for a good grade, choose an alternative way of celebrating. Spend some quality time with your child like take a walk, go to the bowling alley, play a game of cards, or go on a long bike ride together.

Watch what your child drinks, too. Drinks with calories provide lots of sugar with little health benefit. Limit fruit juice to 120-180 gm daily for children ages 1 through 6, and less than 360 gm everyday for older children. Although juice is 'natural' and considered healthy, too much juice, including sweet fruit drinks that are fortified with vitamins and minerals, can be a major source of excess calories in a child's diet.

Be wary of diet soda, as well. Diet soda has zero calories or sugar, but it also has no nutritional value. It is important to remember that juices and sodas may take the place of other nourishing beverages like milk, which is a major source of calcium needed for growing bones.

Do not be too restrictive. Sweets and fast foods do not have to be completely eliminated. They should just make up a very small part of your child's overall diet. Also, do not put your child on a diet unless recommended by your child's doctor—too few calories can interfere with proper growth.

Limit television, video, and computer time. 'There is a clear link between television time—especially when combined with eating—and obesity,' says Dr. Fischer. 'Children should not have television in their bedrooms, and they should limit television, video or computer game time to not more than an hour or two a day.'

Focus on positive goals. 'Overweight children should focus on achieving goals they want to achieve,' says Dr. Fischer. 'They may set their sights on running laps with, instead of behind, the class, or being able to bike for more than 20 minutes without getting tired. It is much better to choose these kinds of positive goals than to focus on more negative-sounding goals, like losing weight.'

Take small steps as a family. Make sure changes are

subtle and involve the whole family. It is better to substitute fruit in place of dessert than to omit dessert altogether. That way your child will not feel like there has been a revolution. Other examples of subtle changes you can make include parking your car a little farther away, not picking up fast food as often, and taking a family walk in the evenings.

As a parent, you must not only confirm the existence of obesity by referring to the height-weight chart provided at the beginning of this book, but also make a note of the amount of weight the child is overweight by. This would help in drawing up a constructive plan in battling childhood obesity.

A healthy and balanced diet

Parents concerned about their child's weight should encourage a variety of fresh, nutritious foods in her diet.

Starchy foods, which are rich in 'complex carbohydrates', are bulky relative to the amount of calories they contain. This makes them filling and nutritious. Sources such as bread, potato, pasta, rice, and chapatti should provide half the energy in a child's diet.

Instead of high-fat foods like chocolate, biscuits, cakes and crisps, try healthier alternatives such as fresh fruits, crusty breads or crackers.

Try to grill or bake food instead of frying. Burgers, fish fingers, and sausages are just as tasty when grilled, and have a lower fat content. Oven chips are lower in fat than fried chips.

Avoid fizzy drinks that are high in sugar. Substitute them with fresh juices diluted with water or sugar-free alternatives.

A healthy breakfast of a low-sugar cereal (for example, wholemeal wheat biscuits) with milk, plus a piece of fruit is a good start to the day.

Instead of sweets, offer dried fruit or tinned fruit in natural juice. Frozen yoghurt is an alternative to ice cream. Bagels are an alternative to doughnuts.

Changes to eating habits

Try to set a good example with your own eating habits.

- Provide meals and snacks at regular times to prevent 'grazing' throughout the day.
- Do not allow your children to eat while watching television or doing homework.
- Make mealtimes an occasion by eating as a family group as often as possible.
- Encourage children to 'listen to their tummies' and eat when they are hungry rather than out of habit.

- Teach your children to chew and savour the food slowly. They will feel fuller more quickly and be less likely to overeat at mealtimes.
- Do not stock high-fat, high-sugar snack foods in the house.
- Do not make outings for fast foods part of the weekly routine.
- Try to get children involved in preparing food as this will make them more aware of what they are eating.
- When children, who need to improve their eating habits, are old enough, it may help them to keep a food diary, recording what and when they eat. It is important to be aware of snacking 'danger times' and find strategies to divert attention away from food, or towards a healthier option.

Physical activity

- Doctors recommend a gradual increase in physical activity, such as brisk walking, to at least an hour a day.
- Encourage walking to places such as school and shops, rather than always taking the car.
- Suggest going to the park to play football, cricket or frisbee.

- Visit a local leisure centre to investigate sports and team activities to get involved in.
- Make exercise into a treat by taking special trips to an adventure play park or an ice skating rink, for example. Involve the whole family in bike rides, swimming, and in-line skating. When it is safe to do so, teach your child to ride a bike.

Reducing physical inactivity

'Physical inactivity' includes pastimes such as watching television or playing computer games. These should be reduced to not more than two hours a day or an average of 14 hours a week.

Encourage children to be selective about what they watch, concentrate only on the programmes they really enjoy.

The emotional factors

Food can take on emotional significance when used to comfort or reward children.

Do not use food to comfort a child—give attention, listening and hugs instead.

Avoid using food as a reward as this can reinforce the idea of food as a source of comfort. Instead of having a fast-food meal to celebrate a good school report, for example, buy a gift, go to the cinema, or have a friend stay overnight.

Prevention

Studies show that breastfeeding a baby, even if only for a short period of time, may reduce the risk of obesity in later life.

Parents who enjoy a healthy diet with plenty of fresh fruit and vegetables set a good example for their children. As children grow older they tend to stick to the eating pattern that has been established at home.

Communication

Most overweight kids are fully aware of their weight. They have likely faced taunts and name-calling at school long before you thought to intervene. So do not be afraid to bring up the topic of health and fitness, but do be sensitive that your child may interpret your concern as an insult.

'Talk to your kids directly, openly and without judgment,' says Dr. Fischer. 'See what they think. Help them set positive goals and work with them to meet those goals.'

By modelling healthy-living habits, staying positive and above all letting your child know that she is loved no matter what, you will find it much easier to help your child lose weight without damaging her self-esteem.

Table Manners

'Do not talk and eat at the same time.'

'Chew from one side of your mouth.'

'Do not wolf down your food.'

'The fork goes in your left hand.'

'The table napkin belongs on your lap not your head!'

'Do not open your mouth while chewing.'

'Your elbows are not part of the cutlery.
Take them off the table!'

Most of us need not have attended finishing school to hear these phrases shouted out at us in a less than polite manner, sometimes even in dictatorial fashion, when we were children. In this book, when talking about table manners for children, we are tackling just the basics and not how to have your child arrange her spoon and fork when waiting to be served.

Generally speaking, a child should have basic table manners by the time she is six years old. This would imply that she should be in a position to eat meals independently (Read: Without coercion or persuasion) with or without appropriate implements and that all of it ought not to look excessively messy.

If you have reached satisfactory levels of etiquette vis-à-vis your child's culinary habits, then you need not read any further. Otherwise read on!

Table manners go a long way in creating the right atmosphere for children to pick up good habits. Children begin to view a meal as an activity that requires attention instead of thinking of meals as something that gets in the way of activity.

Lesson 1: Respect food

Children must know that a meal is something special and that the more attention and respect they give to it, the more they would benefit from it. Try to find out who it is that your child really admires and try and drive a connection between them. For example, the proverbial can of spinach with Popeye.

Lesson 2: Benefit from food

Each food item on the table has one or more benefits. For example, carrot is good for the eyes; milk is good for building strong bones, etc. Incentives that hold promise of growth, strength and / or intelligence are often compelling enough for children to go for the bait.

Lesson 3: Importance of hygiene

This lesson, not surprisingly, might take a little longer than others for you to inculcate in your child. After all, it is their time for experimentation and exploration and children are likely to leave behind the lessons learnt at home when around their friends. So you as a parent just have to try harder and be patient. And also ensure that a high level of hygiene is maintained within your home.

EQ

Let us start off by discussing what is EQ?

It is the ability of a person to handle his or her own feelings and the sensitivity with which one treats those of other people.

So if your child has a high EQ she will be able to cope with her feelings better, calm herself down, and understand and relate well to the adults and other kids around. Research has also shown that kids with a high EQ are more likely to form strong friendships and succeed in school than others. Also, they are better equipped at controlling negative impulses, even when things are not going their way! Experts in child psychology believe that emotional skills can be taught at an early age, when children are more flexible in their inner growth.

How best can a parent impart emotional intelligence?

Parents need to be in tune with their children completely. They have to be able to look out and treat opportunities such as anger, sadness or frustration for the emotion coaching times.

Also, children do not always tell you what is going on in their lives and in their heads. So if your child seems disturbed, sad or upset for no obvious reason, it is wise to look at the bigger picture and think of what might be troubling her. For example, has her school been changed? Did you and your spouse have a bitter argument within earshot of your child? Now these are just a few examples but the best way to tackle these situations is a good sincere talk where it would require you to apologize and redeem the situation if possible.

Take care of not accidentally aggravating the current situation. You would need to be patient and in control.

These moments could also be beneficial for looking at opportunities for intimacy and teaching. You can use all your child's feelings, negative as well as positive, in teaching her how to deal constructively with her emotions. Try not to dismiss her feelings with casual statements such as 'that cat was getting old anyway'. What the child may learn, though is that her feelings are not seen as important. Rather than minimizing her feeling, try and listen and sympathize, even if it makes you anxious or uncomfortable. A better statement would be 'it's hard when a pet dies, isn't it?'

Listen carefully to your child, then mirror back to her what she has said, naming the emotions. For example, your child might be dejected that her next-door neighbours have refused to play with her. If the father responds by telling her to be a big kid and just forget about it, his daughter will most likely think that she is a big baby and deserves not to have any friends. Now it would be much better if the father would have an open discussion by simply saying, 'I bet that hurt your feelings.' His daughter will feel relieved that her father understands what she is feeling and does not think the emotions are out of place. It also gives her an opportunity to talk about the situation and think about what she might do to change things.

To prevent your child from feeling isolated in her sting of depressions you could use examples from your own life to show that you do understand what she has said.

Helping her find words to express her emotions would be a great start. Kids have trouble expressing what they feel. You can also let your child know that it is natural to have conflicting emotions about something for instance, she may both be excited and scared during her first week at school.

Part of helping your child solve problems is establishing clear limits on her behaviour, then guiding her toward a solution. For example, 'I know you are angry with your little brother, but you cannot hit him.' What could you do instead? Give her a set of options to choose from. It has been advised that telling your child to first check his tummy, jaw, and fists to see if they are tight, breathing deeply would help. It would help her regain control again.

You can also encourage your child to talk about why she is angry by drawing out pictures or acting out the story of her madness with toys.

The Mind of the Adolescent Eater

If your child is not all that keen on meals, look closer and you might read his mind and in all probability this is what you will hear.

'I was having fun, so much fun, and then I heard a voice. Oh no, that time of the day again. I wonder why people eat. Why can't all of them have fun instead of food.'

A lot of children are not really sensitive to their hunger pangs. Instead, hunger reflects in a sudden change of mood, long periods of silence or sleep. Some children might snack on the side. As a parent, it is important to make a mental note of these events because if your child, like a great majority of children, has a problem eating meals, then these events hold the key to reaching out and successfully enforcing healthy changes.

Most children love high fat and sugar diets for obvious reasons. They are highly attractive and tasty, easily available in a wide variety and they are increasingly being targetted at children through television advertising. But let us face it, children are not the only ones having problems keeping temptation out of their lives. Adults too have their fair share of indulgence, however, that is well outside the purview of this book.

Children think differently from adults, so one should realize, that it might be difficult for them to share their enthusiasm about health and nutrition. Approach with caution and do not act high handed or forceful about anything. Try and be as receptive to your child's thought processes to know its mechanism.

Identify a pattern in the eating cycles of your child. Make a note of the time in the day when your child feels hungry. How does it differ from holidays and normal/school days? It may well be that your child's appetite increases during exam times probably due to the anxiety she feels. These are the small details that you would need to collate to build the right diet plan, all year round, for your child.

Home Cooking Safety Tips

When we were young, we were told to wash our hands on a regular basis, especially before eating. We were told to keep our nails short, taught not to eat food that had fallen on the floor, and a host of do's and don'ts to keep ourselves clean. However, cleanliness is a very relative term. When cleanliness is seen against the backdrop of safe and unsafe, the concept of hygiene takes form.

Hygienic cooking is largely responsible for maintaining good health for you and your family and its importance cannot be overstated. After all, a great majority of all infections are food-borne illnesses.

The importance of hygiene is even more when talking of a child. Children, by and large, have a weaker immune system when compared to the average, healthy adult.

Here are few basic concepts to hygienic cooking:

Clean hands

Clean hands are the first important step towards ensuring an adequate level of hygiene. Try and keep your nails short, if nails need to be maintained at a certain length, consider using disposable gloves. Wash your hands with soap and warm water before handling food items. Make it a habit to wash your hands after opening doors, receiving phone calls, and making physical contact with any object that might contain microbes.

Clean all the cooking implements

Knives, chopping boards, spoons, forks, and all the utensils must be washed before use. If they have been washed the previous day, then at least a rinse with warm water is required before using them. After use, wash the cooking implements and let them dry before keeping them back. Also remember to wash and change aprons and dusting cloth on a regular basis.

Clean storage and refrigeration

Refrigeration does not kill the bacteria in food, it only stops the bacteria from multiplying. This drastically slows down the rate of degeneration in refrigerated foodstuffs allowing them to be stored for consumption over extended periods of time. It is advisable, however, to defrost and clean your refrigerator at least once a week. If you have a frost-free refrigerator, it is advisable to re-arrange all foodstuffs in the fridge at least once a fortnight. By doing this, you will reduce the chances of cross-contamination in addition to allowing refrigerated items to stay fresh for longer.

If you are following these guidelines you have already created the right platform to ward off the sources of a good majority of food-borne illnesses. There is more, however, in this battle against food-borne diseases.

Info capsule

A recent survey conducted by the Food Marketing Institute revealed that a shocking 68 per cent of people do not wash their hands after using the washroom. Now before you run off trying to wash every inch of your house that others might have touched, here are few tips to ensure that you do not allow other people to threaten the health of your family:

- Inculcate the habit of washing hands before a meal in your family.

- Clean the doorknobs or door handles in the house on a weekly basis.
- Dissuade your children from playing on the floor, especially those parts on which people walk with their shoes.
- Consider allocating a playing area outside your child's bedroom to entertain her friends.
- When with friends for a meal at home, politely ask them whether they would like to use the washroom to wash up. If that is inappropriate, consider using hand towels dampened in mild antiseptic water.

Beware that these habits do not turn into a fetish. Psychological conditions like OCD or Obsessive Compulsive Disorder are often due to such a fetish. These conditions are often very traumatic and take a long time of psychiatric therapy to heal. Therefore, try and steer away from using fear or anger and thus scaring your children into keeping themselves clean. Consider using a more scientific approach: initiate a discussion on hygiene and its importance and then suggest the importance of clean hands.

Till now, we have discussed the obvious, the tangible in a sense, while talking of food safety. Now let us look at the not so obvious:

Cross-contamination

Cross-contamination is one such phenomenon, which is far less obvious to the naked eye. It occurs when juices from meat mix with those from vegetables or fruit. When you use a chopping board to slice pieces of meat, and then use the same chopping board (without thoroughly washing it) to dice salad, there is a good chance that the salad is contaminated with bacteria from the meat. Using two separate chopping boards, one for meat and the other for vegetables and fruit could resolve such a problem. It is still mandatory that you wash your boards before and after cutting.

Here are a few pointers that go a long way in preventing cross-contamination:

- After washing produce, place them in clean storage containers, not in the original bags they came from.
- If your hand is cut or you have an open wound, consider using disposable gloves while handling produce.
- Use a fresh spoon every time you need to taste the food being prepared.
- Ensure that you wash the knives between uses or use separate knives for non-vegetarian and vegetarian items.

- Store meat and vegetables and fruits in different locations such that the meat products cannot contaminate the fruit and vegetable produce by dripping on to them.
- Consume leftover food within 2-3 days.

Another aspect of maintaining a high level of hygiene is, obviously, taking appropriate measures while preparing the food to prevent contamination. That would mean, heating the food to an appropriate temperature and ensuring that all the foodstuffs being used have not gone bad.

Drinks and Beverages

Almond milk

Preparation time: 10 min. Serves: 1

Ingredients:

Almonds (*badaam*), soaked overnight in 1 cup water	10
Milk	1 cup
Sugar to taste	

Method:

1. Drain and peel the almonds. Cut each almond into 3 pieces.
2. Bring the milk to the boil in a pan. Add the almonds and sugar to taste; mix well. Serve hot.

This drink can also be served chilled in the hot summer months. It is an energy booster.

Banana Orange Smoothie

Preparation time: 5 min. Serves: 2

Ingredients:

Banana (*kela*), peeled	1
Orange (*santra*), peeled, pitted	1
Vanilla-flavoured soya milk	2 cups
Ginger (*adrak*), ground	1 tsp

Method:

1. Put all the ingredients in an electric blender. Process until well blended and smooth.
2. Serve chilled, topped with ice.

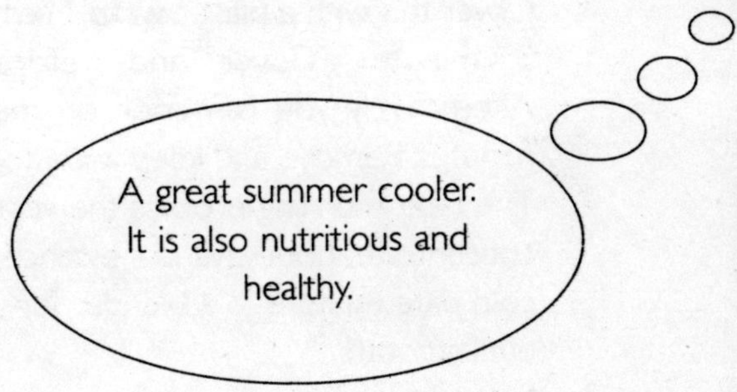

Blended Sunrise

Preparation time: 10 min. Serves: 2

Ingredients:

Water	1/4 cup
Dates (*khajoor*), pitted	8
Plain non-fat yoghurt (*dahi*)	2 cups
Frozen orange juice concentrate (Rasna)	1/4 cup
Honey	1 tbsp
Vanilla essence	1 tsp
Banana (*kela*), medium-sized, peeled	1

Method:

1. Mix the water with the dates in a micro-safe cup. Cover this with a plastic wrap. Microwave on high for 3 minutes. Cover and refrigerate overnight. Alternatively, you can cook on medium heat for 6 minutes. Remove and keep aside to cool. Refrigerate.
2. The next morning process the yoghurt, orange juice concentrate, honey, vanilla essence, banana, and the cold date mixture in a blender for 30-60 seconds or until smooth.
3. Serve immediately.

Juicy Date Shake

Preparation time: 5 min. Serves: 2

Ingredients:

Dates (*khajoor*), pitted	6
Soya milk or milk	1 1/2 cups
Vanilla essence	1/2 tsp
Coconut (*nariyal*), shredded, unsweetened	1/2 cup

Method:

1. Blend all the ingredients together till smooth.
2. Serve immediately, as the coconut will settle down.

This is an excellent digestive drink, sweet and cooling at the same time. You could experiment with a bit of cardamom or cloves if you wish for extra digestibility.

Hot Ginger Tea

Preparation and Cooking time: 15 min. Serves: 1

Ingredients:

Ginger (*adrak*), peeled, mashed, 1″ piece	1
Water	1 1/2 cups
Lemon (*nimbu*) juice	1/2 tsp
Honey or to taste	1 tsp

Method:

1. Bring the water to the boil. Reduce heat and let it simmer. Add ginger and boil covered, so that the vapour does not escape. The more it boils the stronger the potency.
2. After 8 minutes, strain and add lemon juice and honey. Serve hot.

This drink is an effective remedy for running nose, mild sore throat, bronchitis or even poor digestion.

Hot Nutmeg Milk

Preparation and Cooking time: 10 min. Serves: 1

Ingredients:

Milk	1 cup
Nutmeg (*jaiphal*), powdered	1/2 tsp

Method:

1. Bring the milk to the boil; reduce heat and add nutmeg. Simmer for 5-6 minutes. Remove and strain.
2. Serve hot.

This is a good remedy to relieve children from stress during exams or sleeping disorder.

Iron-rich Breakfast Drink

Preparation time: 5 min. + overnight soaking
Serves: 1

Ingredients:

Raisins (*kishmish*)	1/4 cup
Apricot or peaches, dried	1/4 cup
Water	1 cup
Dry ginger (*sonth*) powder	a pinch

Method:

1. Soak the dried fruits in water overnight.
2. The next morning, blend the fruits along with the water and dry ginger powder. Serve immediately.

Variation:

Add 1 cup yoghurt to the drink and mix well. This drink is an excellent digestive aid and toner. It is also mildly laxative in nature.

Serve this drink early in the morning. It is effective if your child is a bit under the weather, anaemic or requires a spurt of instant energy for the day.

Maple Syrup Shake

Preparation time: 10-15 min. Serves: 4

Ingredients:

Milk	4 cups
Honey	3 tbsp
Ice, crushed	1 cup
Vanilla ice cream	2 scoops
Maple syrup	3/5 cup

Method:

Blend all the ingredients together in a mixer till smooth. Serve chilled.

Honey should be included in the child's diet in various forms as it not only has rejuvenating properties, but also has antiseptic and antibacterial properties.

Pistachio Milk

Preparation and Cooking time: 15 min. Serves: 2

Ingredients:

Milk	2 cups
Green cardamom (*choti elaichi*), powdered	5
Cornflour	3 tsp
Sugar to taste	
Pistachios (*pista*), shelled, chopped into small pieces	20
Almonds (*badaam*), chopped into small pieces	25
Vanilla essence	a drop
Vanilla ice cream	2 scoops

Method:

1. Boil the milk in a saucepan. Add cardamom powder.
2. Mix the cornflour with a little water to make a smooth paste. Add to the boiling milk.
3. Stir in the sugar. Remove. Let the mixture cool before placing it in the refrigerator to chill.
4. When sufficiently cool, add the pistachios and almonds; blend in a mixi. Add vanilla essence, mix and refrigerate. When serving, top with half a scoop of vanilla ice cream.

Honeyed Milk

Preparation and Cooking time: 5 min. Serves: 2

Ingredients:

Milk	2 cups
Honey	2 tbsp

Method:

1. Mix the milk and honey together, bring to the boil in a saucepan.
2. Remove and pour into mugs. Serve warm.

This drink is an instant stomachache reliever. The child could be suffering from mild indigestion or muscle cramps after playing. The drink soothes the nerves and calms the muscles. Best had at bed time.

Soothing Milk

Preparation time: 10 min. Serves: 4-5

Ingredients:

Milk	2 1/4 cups
Water	1 1/2 cups
Aniseed (*saunf*)	2 tsp
Cumin (*jeera*) seeds	2 tsp
Mustard seeds (*rai*)	3/4 tsp
Poppy seeds (*khus khus*)	1 1/2 tsp
Green cardamom (*choti elaichi*)	7
Black peppercorns (*sabut kali mirch*)	2 tsp
Cumin powder	2 tsp
Almonds (*badaam*) / Cashew nuts (*kaju*)	20
Sugar	12 tsp
Ice, crushed	5 tsp

Method:

1. Dry grind aniseed, cumin seeds, mustard seeds, poppy seeds, green cardamom, and black peppercorns together to a fine powder and transfer to a bowl.
2. Grind the almonds / cashew nuts and mix with the ground spice.

3. Mix the milk and water with the spice mixture thoroughly.
4. Strain the juice through a muslin or thin cloth. Repeat this process till you find that all the fluid has been strained through.
5. Stir in the sugar and crushed ice. Serve chilled.

This is an extremely soothing and cooling drink for all during the summers. It settles down the digestive tract and also mildly increases the appetite, which is a little low during summers. It is an energy booster.

Wake Up Shake

Preparation time: 10 min. Serves: 3

Ingredients:

Bananas (*kela*), medium-sized, ripe, peeled, sliced	2
Low-fat milk or skimmed milk	1 1/4 cups
Frozen berries or peaches	1 cup
Cottage cheese (*paneer*)	1/2 cup
Ice cubes, large	5
Strawberries, fresh for garnishing	

Method:

1. Wrap the banana slices in a foil and freeze them overnight.
2. The next morning, mix the frozen bananas with the milk, berries, and cottage cheese. Blend till the consistency is smooth. Add ice, cover and blend again.
3. Transfer the mixture to a pitcher and refrigerate or serve immediately. Top with fresh strawberries, if desired.

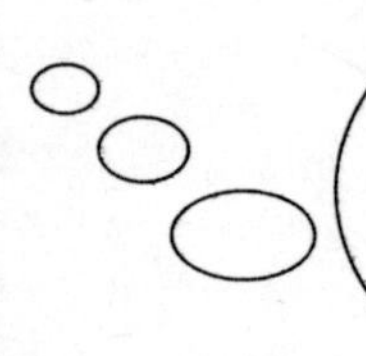

This is a thick shake.
Children love this during the summer months when it gets too hot to eat and they need hydration and energy to cope with the heat.

Snacks and Starters

Banana Bread

Preparation and Cooking time: 1 1/2 hrs. Serves: 3

Ingredients:

Bananas (*kela*), mashed	3
All purpose flour (*maida*)	1 1/2 cups
Baking soda	1 tsp
Salt	1/2 tsp
Sugar	1 cup
Eggs, slightly beaten	2
Butter, melted	1/4 cup

Method:

1. Grease and flour two 7" x 3" loaf pans. Preheat oven to 180°C / 350°F.
2. Mix the flour, baking soda, salt, and sugar together in a bowl. Blend in the eggs, melted butter, and mashed bananas. Pour the batter into the prepared pans. Bake for 1 hour or until a wooden toothpick inserted in the centre comes out clean.
3. Serve hot with vanilla ice cream, if you like.

Banana Hot Dogs

Preparation time: 10 min. Serves: 2-4

Ingredients:

Hot dog buns	2-4
Salted butter	
Banana (*kela*), ripe	2-3
Honey to taste	

Method:

1. Slice the bananas and keep them aside on a plate. Take the hot dog bread (split into two) and spread some butter over on both sides.
2. Add the banana slices inside. You can put 2-3 slices per hot dog. Pour the honey over it and cover with the other half of the bread.

An easy-to-make-snack. Encourage your child to make it himself / herself. You could also add some crushed cashew nuts over the honey for an additional zing!

Brown Bread Sandwich

Preparation time: 10 min. Serves: 2-4

Ingredients:

Brown bread	2-4 slices
Peanut butter	2 tbsp
Jam (of your choice)	
Bananas (*kela*), honey, dried fruit	

Method:

1. Spread peanut butter on one slice of bread and jam on the other to make a sandwich.
2. Add bananas or honey or dried fruit depending on what your child prefers.

A good way to recognize pure honey is by keeping the jar in the fridge. If the consistency remains thick, then the honey is pure. But if it forms crystals it's definitely not genuine.

Cheese Deluxe

Preparation and Cooking time: 15 min. Serves: 4

Ingredients:

Swiss cheese, shredded	120 gm
Cheddar cheese, shredded	120 gm
Mayonnaise	1/3 cup
Mustard	1 tbsp
Spring onion (*hara pyaz*), chopped	1 tbsp
Bread	8 slices
Butter, softened	1/4 cup
Oregano	1 tsp

Method:

1. Mix both the cheeses, mayonnaise, mustard, and spring onion together.
2. Spread the mixture on one side of the bread slice. Top with another slice of bread. Spread some butter on top of the sandwich. Cook on medium heat in a hot skillet or griddle until golden brown, turning once. Repeat with the other slices.
3. Sprinkle some oregano and serve.

Cream Cheese Roll Ups

Preparation time: 5 min. Serves: 8

Ingredients:

Cream cheese	240 gm
Mayonnaise	1/3 cup
Pitted green olives	2/3 cup
Black olives	1/2 cup
Spring onions (*hara pyaz*), chopped	8
Tortillas (available in the market)	8
Salsa (available in the market)	1/2 cup

Method:

1. Mix the cream cheese, mayonnaise, green olives, black olives, and spring onions together in a bowl. Spread the cream cheese mixture in a fine layer over each tortilla. Roll up the tortillas. Chill for about an hour, or till you find that the filling is firm.
2. Slice these chilled roll ups into 1″ pieces and serve with salsa.

Edible Face

Preparation time: 5-8 min. Serves: 1-2

Ingredients:

Cheddar cheese	30 gm
Cherry tomatoes, halved	2
Thin wheat crackers	8
Carrots (*gajar*), shredded	1/4 cup
Orange, peeled, segmented	1

Method:

1. Slice the cheese into shapes (could be triangles, squares or circles). Place the cheese shapes and cherry tomato halves on the crackers. Use your imagination to make faces complete with eyes, nose, ears, mouth, and hair with the shredded carrot and orange segments. Your children will enjoy them.
2. You could also involve your kids in this game.

French Fried Tomatoes

Preparation and Cooking time: 15 min. Serves: 3

Ingredients:

Tomatoes, firm, washed	4
Salt	1 tsp
Black pepper (*kali mirch*)	1/8 tsp
Sugar	1 tsp
Egg, slightly beaten	1
Milk	1/4 cup
Breadcrumbs for coating	

Method:

1. Cut the tomatoes into 1″-thick pieces. Dust them with salt, black pepper, and sugar. Dip the slices in egg mixed with milk.
2. Roll the tomato pieces over the breadcrumbs.
3. Heat the oil in a pan; fry the tomato pieces for 5 seconds or till the breadcrumb turns brown. Remove and drain the excess oil on absorbent paper towels. Serve warm.

A delicious snack for children after school.

Sliced Eggplant

Preparation and Cooking time: 20 min. Serves: 2

Ingredients:

Eggplant (*baingan*), medium-sized, washed	2
Vegetable oil	1 tbsp
Breadcrumbs	3 tbsp
Salt to taste	
Black pepper (*kali mirch*)	1 tsp

Method:

1. Pat-dry the eggplant. With a sharp knife cut them into thin round slices.
2. Heat the oil in a skillet; coat each slice with breadcrumbs and fry slightly on medium heat for 5-7 minutes or till brown on both sides.
3. Serve hot sprinkled with salt and black pepper.

Chopped eggplant discolours quickly due to its high iron content, to prevent it put it in a bowl of water.

Mostly Toasted

Preparation time: 10 min. Serves: 4

Ingredients:

White bread	4 slices
Eggs	2
Milk	4 tbsp
Salt and black pepper (*kali mirch*) to taste	
Butter	a little
Tomato ketchup to taste	

Method:

1. Toast the bread in a toaster or in a saucepan on medium heat with a little oil.
2. In a small bowl whisk the eggs with milk. Add salt and black pepper.
3. In another pan, heat a little butter and scramble your egg batter. In the meantime, cut a slice of toast into 4 pieces and place a bit of the scrambled egg on each quarter. Top it off with a bit of tomato ketchup. Repeat with the other quarters.

This can be served as a quick snack in a kid's birthday party or as a breakfast item. Serve hot.

Hasty Tasty Haystacks

Preparation time: 25 min. Serves: 6

Ingredients:

Kidney beans (*rajma*), cooked	2 cups
Salt	1 tsp
Red chilli powder	2 tbsp
Black pepper (*kali mirch*), ground	1 tsp
Corn tortilla chips	1 packet
Iceberg lettuce, shredded	1 head
Tomatoes, large	2
Green pepper (*Shimla mirch*)	1
Carrot (*gajar*)	1
Cheddar cheese, shredded	1 cup
Onion, chopped	1
Black olives	1 cup
Salsa (available in the market)	1 cup
Sour cream	1/2 cup

Method:

1. Heat the cooked kidney beans along with the salt, red chilli powder, and black pepper till its warm enough.
2. Take a handful of the corn chips on a plate, add 1 tbsp of the heated bean mixture, and garnish with lettuce, tomato, green pepper, onion, carrot, and cheddar cheese. Top the haystack with sour cream and salsa. Serve with white or brown bread.

Potato Cheese Balls

Preparation and Cooking time: 40 min. Serves: 2-4

Ingredients:

Potatoes, large	2
Cheese spread (unflavoured)	2 tbsp
Salt to taste	
Green coriander (*hara dhaniya*), chopped	1 tbsp

Method:

1. Boil the potatoes. Peel and mash with a fork.
2. In a bowl, mix the mashed potatoes with the remaining ingredients. With dry hands, divide the mixture into small balls. Refrigerate for half and hour or till it binds.
3. Serve.

If you are in a hurry and need to serve these quickly, instead of refrigerating, you could lightly fry the potato cheese balls in 1 tbsp oil in a non-stick pan.

Egg Spread

Preparation time: 20 min. Makes: 4 sandwiches

Ingredients:

Eggs, hard-boiled	4
Mayonnaise	3 tbsp
Black pepper (*kali mirch*)	1/4 tsp
Salt	1/2 tsp

Method:

1. Remove the shells and mash the eggs with a fork. Mix the remaining ingredients in a bowl.
2. Combine the above with any one of these: 1/4 cup minced celery, 2 tbsp minced onion and 2 tbsp chilli sauce. Or you can also mix 2 tbsp minced pickles, 1 tsp prepared mustard, and 1 tsp minced onion. Or 1 tbsp minced green bell pepper, 1 tbsp chopped pimento, and 1 tsp chilli powder.

This can also be served on cream or cheese crackers and of course, it makes a great sandwich spread.

Egg Salad

Preparation time: 20 min. Serves: 1-2

Ingredients:

Eggs, hard-boiled	2
Mayonnaise	1 tbsp
Mustard, ground	1 tsp

Salt and black pepper (*kali-mirch*) to taste

Paprika and green coriander (*hara dhaniya*) for garnishing

Method:

1. Hard-boil the eggs. Remove the shells and mash the eggs with a fork.
2. Mix all the ingredients into the mashed eggs and garnish with paprika and coriander.

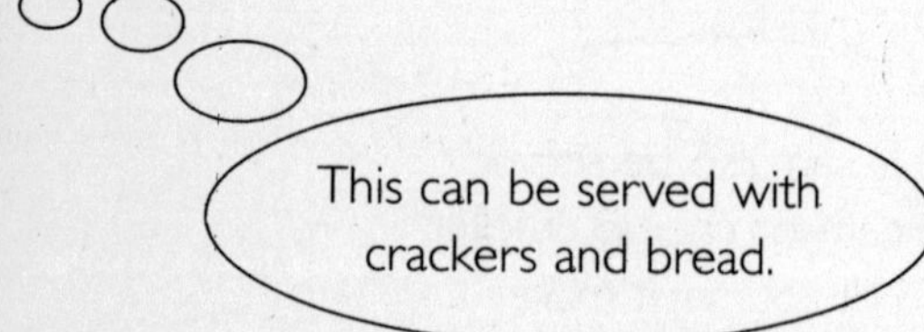

Eggless Egg Salad

Preparation time: 10 min. Serves: 4-5

Ingredients:

Eggless mayonnaise	2 tbsp
Sweet pickle relish	1 tbsp
White vinegar (*sirka*)	1 tbsp
Mustard paste	1 tsp
Sugar	1 tsp
Turmeric (*haldi*) powder	1/2 tsp
Dry dill weed	1/4 tsp
Dried parsley	1 tbsp
Tofu, firm, sliced, drained	450 gm
Onion, minced	1 tbsp
Celery, minced	2 tbsp
Salt and black pepper (*kali mirch*) to taste	

Method:

1. Combine the eggless mayonnaise with sweet pickle relish, vinegar, mustard paste, sugar, turmeric powder, dill, and parsley in a bowl. Mix well, and keep aside.
2. Place the drained tofu in a large bowl, and break it with a fork. Stir in the onion and celery. Mix in the reserved mixture. Add salt and pepper to taste.
3. Chill for a few hours to allow the juices and flavours to blend. Serve on wholewheat toast with fresh crisp lettuce and tomato slices.

Flip Flop Egg

Preparation and Cooking time: 8 min. Serves: 1

Ingredients:

Egg	1
Butter	1 tsp
Milk	2 tsp
Cheddar cheese	1 slice

Method:

1. Melt the butter in a small skillet on medium heat.
2. Whisk the egg and milk in a bowl and pour into the skillet. Cook until bubbles appear then flip over. Add cheese and cook for about 10 seconds or till the cheese melts. Serve hot.

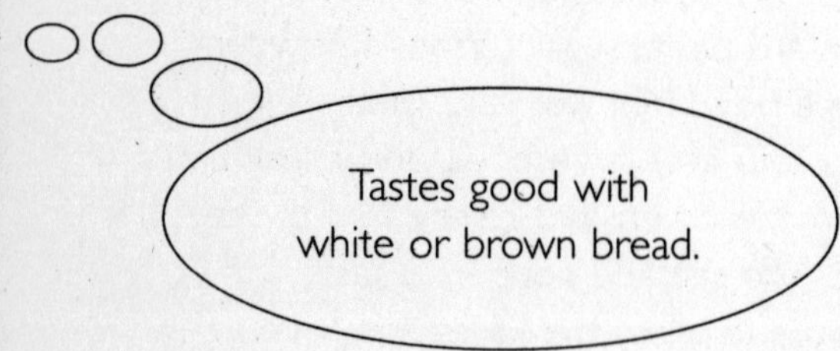

Fried Tomatoes 'n' Eggs

Preparation and Cooking time: 15 min. Serves: 2

Ingredients:

Tomatoes, medium-sized, chopped into quarters	2
Eggs	2
Vegetable oil	2 tbsp
Black pepper (*kali mirch*) to taste	
Salt to taste	
Green chilli, chopped (optional)	1
Green coriander (*hara dhaniya*)	a small bunch

Method:

1. Heat the oil in a flat pan on medium heat; add the tomatoes and sprinkle black pepper and salt to taste.
2. Add the green chilli, if using, and stir-fry for about 2-3 minutes. Move the contents to one side of the pan and manoeuvre the excess oil to the other side of the pan. Break the two eggs in the oil and fry. Sprinkle salt and pepper on the eggs and garnish with green coriander.
3. Serve with brown bread.

Use juicy red tomatoes so as to allow the juices to mix with the eggs.

Steamed Eggs

Preparation and Cooking time: 15 min. Serves: 4

Ingredients:

Eggs	4
Butter	a little
Cumin (*jeera*) seeds	1/4 tsp
Garlic (*lasan*), chopped	a little
Onions, finely chopped	2
Tomatoes, finely chopped	2

Salt and black pepper (*kali mirch*) to taste
Green coriander (*hara dhaniya*), chopped for garnishing

Method:

1. Heat the butter in a medium-sized skillet with a heavy bottom and a top; add the cumin seeds and garlic. When the seeds begin to pop, add onions and sauté until it gets a bit pink.
2. Add the tomatoes and mix in the salt and pepper (you can also add green coriander as this adds colour and freshness to the taste). Reduce heat and centre all the cooked ingredients in the pan. Carefully break the eggs, one by one, over this mixture. Cover the pan and steam the eggs for about 7 minutes.
3. Open the lid carefully and with a flat spoon take the eggs out without breaking them.
4. Serve hot garnished with green coriander.

Olive Cheese Melts

Preparation and Cooking time: 25 min. Makes: 8

Ingredients:

Black olives, finely chopped	1 cup
Green onions, chopped	1/3 cup
Cheddar cheese, shredded	1 1/2 cups
Curry powder	1/2 tsp
Mayonnaise	1/2 cup
Salt	1/2 tsp
Muffins, split into half	8

Method:

1. Preheat the oven to 200°C / 400°F.
2. Mix the olives, green onions, cheddar cheese, curry powder, mayonnaise, and salt in a bowl. Spread this mixture on the muffins and place the muffin pieces on a cookie sheet and bake at 200°C / 400°F for just 10 minutes. Remove and serve hot.

A delicious snack or breakfast item for your child. A good way of introducing the taste of olives.

Quick Pancakes

Preparation and Cooking time: 15 min. Serves: 2

Ingredients:

Sugar	1 cup
Salt	a pinch
Refined flour (*maida*)	2 cups
Butter	a little
Milk	1 cup

Vegetable oil for frying the pancakes

Method:

1. Mix the sugar, salt, and flour together. Add milk and butter; mix well to make a smooth paste.
2. Heat a little oil in a frying pan; pour a ladleful of batter and cook for 2 minutes or till lightly brown. Flip over gently and cook the other side. Repeat till all the batter is used up.
3. Serve hot with maple syrup or honey.

This will make a delicious and hearty breakfast food.

Eggplant Rice Patties

Preparation time and Cooking time: 1 1/2 hrs. Serves: 6

Ingredients:

Eggplant (*baingan*)	1 cup
Cooked rice	3/4 cup
Egg	1
All purpose flour (*maida*)	2 tbsp
Black pepper (*kali mirch*)	1/4 tsp
Salt	1/2 tsp
Red pepper sauce	a dash
Onion, grated	2 tbsp
Cheddar cheese, grated	1/2 cup
Vegetable oil for frying	

Method:

1. Peel the skin of the eggplant, if you desire, and boil till tender. Drain and mash the cooked eggplant.
2. Mix the remaining ingredients (except oil) with the eggplant. Cover and chill for at least 1 hour.
3. Divide the mixture equally into 6 portions and shape each into a patty.
4. Heat the vegetable oil in a heavy skillet; and when hot place the patties and cook until crispy brown on both sides. Remove and drain the excess oil on absorbent paper towels. Serve at once with tomato sauce or coriander chutney (see p. 92).

Green Potato Patties

Preparation and Cooking time: 45 min. Serves: 5-6

Ingredients:

Potatoes, medium-sized	5
Green peas (*hara muttar*), frozen	3 cups
Vegetable oil	1 tbsp
Mustard seeds (*rai*)	1/2 tsp
Salt	1 1/2 tsp
Lemon (*nimbu*) juice	1 tsp
Sesame (*til*) seeds	1 tsp
Black pepper (*kali mirch*)	1/2 tsp
Red chilli powder	1/2 tsp

Method:

1. Boil the potatoes in 3 cups of water with the skin and keep aside to cool.
2. Blend the green peas to a smooth paste in a blender.
3. Heat the oil in a pan; add the mustard seeds. When the seeds start popping, add the pea paste and 1 tsp salt. Cook for about 10 minutes on low heat or till the water begins to dry up. Remove from heat and mix in lemon juice, sesame seeds, and black pepper.
4. Skin and mash the potatoes. Add red chilli powder and 2 tsp salt. Divide the mixture equally into approximately 14-15 balls and gently flatten them to

about 2 1/2" diameter. Make a groove in the patty and place 1 tbsp of the pea mixture. Fold up the sides to enclose the filling inside. Gently flatten the patty once more. Repeat till all the patties are done.

5. Heat a little oil in a non-stick saucepan; when hot, place a patty in the centre and fry on low heat till one-side browns and then flip it over and repeat with the other side. Remove, and repeat with the other patties. Serve hot garnished with mint leaves.

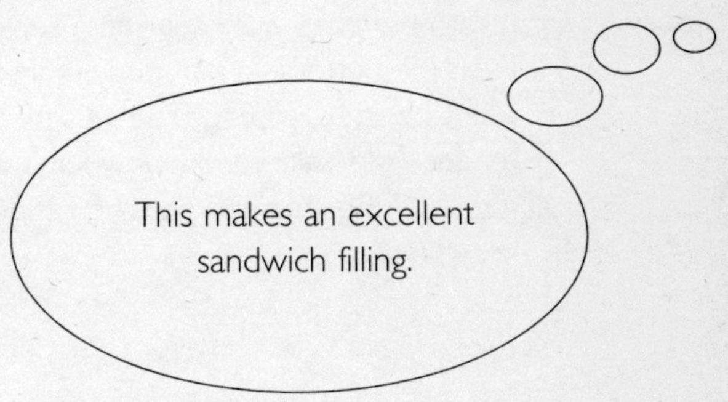

Mushroom and Peas

Preparation and Cooking time: 15 min. Serves: 3-4

Ingredients:

Mushrooms (*gucchi*)	125 gm
Green peas (*hara muttar*), fresh	2 cups
Butter	3 tbsp
Cumin (*jeera*) seeds	1 tsp
Salt	1 tsp
Cumin powder	2 tsp
Black pepper (*kali mirch*), ground	2 tsp

Method:

1. Wash, dry and slice the mushrooms.
2. Steam the peas and keep them separately.
3. Heat the butter in a pan; add cumin seeds. When the seeds begin to pop, add the mushrooms and sauté till tender. Add salt, cumin powder, and black pepper; mix. Add the steamed peas and stir till cooked.
4. Serve hot.

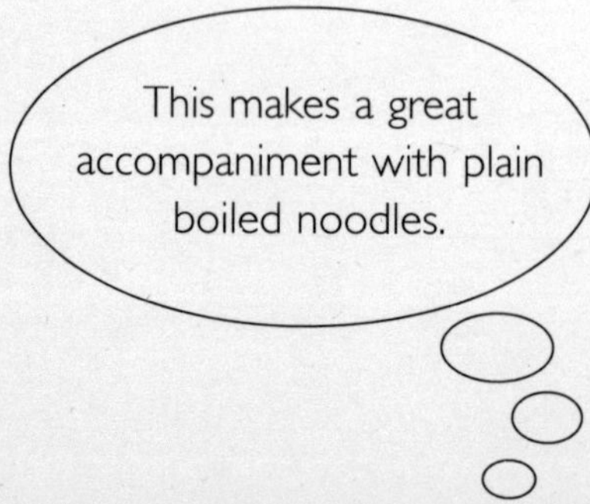

Steamed Sweet Beetroots

Preparation and Cooking time: 30 min. Serves: 4-5

Ingredients:

Beetroots (*chukandar*)	4 cups
Butter, melted	2 tbsp
Lemon (*nimbu*) juice	2 tbsp
Coriander (*dhaniya*) powder	1 tbsp

Method:

1. Wash and slice the beetroots into 1/4" pieces.
2. Pour some water in a heavy skillet, place a stainless steel steamer and bring the water to the boil. Place the beetroot inside the steamer and steam for 20-25 minutes.
3. Transfer to a serving dish, mash the beetroot, add butter and lemon juice. Before serving stir in the coriander powder.

Stewed Figs or Prunes

Preparation time: 15 min. Serves: 2

Ingredients:

Dried figs or prunes	1/4 cup
Boiling water	1 cup

Method:

1. Boil the prunes or figs in a small heatproof vessel, covered. Let this soak for around 10 minutes.
2. Serve.

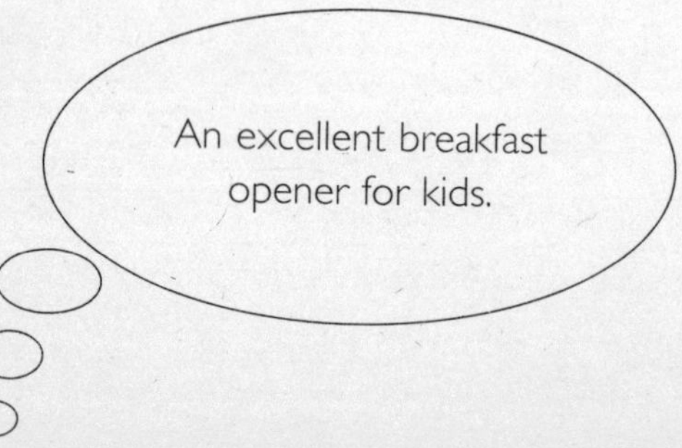

Salted Cashews

Preparation time: 5 min. Serves: 1 cup

Ingredients:

Raw cashew nuts (*kaju*)	1 cup
Salt	1/2-1 tsp
Coriander (*dhaniya*) powder	1 tsp

Method:

Mix all the ingredients together and serve.

It is a great substitute for the commercially available fried nuts and it is also easier to digest. Ideally served as a snack.

Corn 'n' Peanut Balls

Preparation time: 15 min. Serves: 2-4

Ingredients:

Peanut butter	1/2 cup
Corn flakes, crushed (plain ones are preferable)	1 cup
Honey	1/2 cup
Powdered milk	2 tbsp
Corn flakes, crushed for coating	1 tbsp

Method:

1. Mix all the ingredients (leave some crushed flakes aside for coating) together thoroughly. Divide the mixture equally into small balls.
2. Roll the balls over the crushed corn flakes. Serve at room temperature or chilled.

This can turn out to be a yummy snack. Alternatively if you have frozen it, you could then add the balls to cold milk and serve at breakfast!

Sesame Spinach

Preparation and Cooking time: 15 min. Serves: 2

Ingredients:

Spinach (*palak*)	400 gm / 1 bundle
Olive oil	1 tsp
Soya sauce	1/2 tsp
Sugar	1/4 tsp
Vinegar (*sirka*)	1/4 tsp
Sesame (*til*) seeds	a pinch

Method:

1. Rinse and clean the spinach thoroughly in running water. Drain and steam in a non-stick pan for 8 minutes. Leave covered.
2. Mix the remaining ingredients (except the sesame seeds) into a smooth paste.
3. Mix the paste with the spinach and serve garnished with sesame seeds.

You could lightly roast the sesame seeds before garnishing. You could also add a pinch of salt if required. The recipe does not contain salt since spinach intrinsically has a salty taste.

Fresh Coriander Chutney

Preparation time: 5 min. Makes: 1 cup

Ingredients:

Green coriander (*hara dhaniya*)	1 bunch
Lemon (*nimbu*) juice	1/4 cup
Salt	1 tsp
Black pepper (*kali mirch*)	1/4 tsp
Ginger (*adrak*), chopped	2 tbsp
Honey	1 tsp
Water	1/4 cup
Coconut (*nariyal*), grated	1/4 cup

Method:

1. Blend all the ingredients in a mixer and store in the refrigerator.
2. This chutney can be eaten with tortillas, dosa, parathas or anything with which you feel comfortable to experiment with.
3. The chutney can be stored for up to a week in the refrigerator.

You could also add a twig of mint for added zing.

Main Course

Artichokes

Preparation and Cooking time: 50 min. Serves: 3-4

Ingredients:

Artichokes, large	2
Water	3 cups
Salt	1/4 tsp
Bay leaf (*tej patta*)	1

Method:

1. Wash the artichokes and trim off the base.
2. Bring the water to the boil in a large saucepan with salt and bay leaf.
3. Add the artichokes and cook covered on medium heat for 45 minutes or till tender. Alternatively, cook in the pressure cooker for 15 minutes.
4. Remove the artichokes from the water and serve hot.

Bean Burritos

Preparation and Cooking time: 1 hr. Serves: 4-6

Ingredients:

Pinto beans	1/2 cup
Water	6 cups
Onion, medium-sized, chopped	1/2
Garlic (*lasan*) cloves, minced	1-2
Red chilli powder	1-2 tsp
Bay leaf (*tej patta*)	1
Dried oregano	1/2 tsp
Dried basil	1/2 tsp
Cumin (*jeera*) seeds	1/2 tsp
Asafoetida (*hing*)	1/8 tsp
Coriander (*dhaniya*) powder	1 tsp
Spearmint	1 tsp
Salt to taste	

Method:

1. Wash and soak the beans overnight. Drain.
2. Put all the ingredients (except coriander powder, spearmint, and salt) in the cooker and cook at medium heat for 30 minutes.
3. Open the cooker and add the remaining three ingredients and continue to cook for 10 more minutes. Remove and serve with corn or wheat tortillas, corn bread or with a fresh salad.

Burritos

After preparing the beans as mentioned above, heat both sides of a wheat tortilla with 1/2 tsp butter or oil on a heavy skillet. Remove and place the tortilla on a plate and spread the hot beans over it. Roll and secure with a toothpick and serve with rich sour cream or plain cream dip. This would make a great snack or fast lunch or supper.

If salt is added before pressure cooking the beans, they take longer to cook. Bean burritos is high in protein and fibre.

Cajun Red Beans

Preparation and Cooking time: 1 hr. Serves: 4-6

Ingredients:

Dry kidney beans (*rajma*)	2 cups
Water	8 cups
Asafoetida (*hing*)	1/4 tsp
Bay leaves (*tej patta*)	2
Seaweed (optional)	1 stick
Vegetable oil	2 tbsp
Onion, medium-sized, chopped	1/2
Cumin (*jeera*) seeds	1/2 tsp
Thyme, fresh	1 tsp
Neem leaves, crushed	2
Green coriander (*hara dhaniya*), chopped	1 tsp
Jalapeno, small, chopped	1
Salt	1-2 tsp

Method:

1. Pressure cook the kidney beans with water, asafoetida, bay leaves, and seaweed (optional) for about 30 minutes on medium heat.
2. Heat the oil in a skillet; sauté the onion, cumin seeds, thyme, neem, and salt for 1-2 minutes. Keep aside.
3. Add the boiled kidney beans; mix well. Reduce heat, simmer for 20-30 minutes. Garnish with green coriander and jalapeno. Serve with rice or brown bread.

Stir-fried Broccoli and Tofu

Preparation and Cooking time: 20 min. Serves: 4

Ingredients:

For the sauce:

Peanut butter or Almond butter	1/2 cup
Water, hot	1/2 cup
Vinegar (*sirka*)	1/4 cup
Soya sauce	2 tbsp
Blackstrap molasses	2 tbsp
Cayenne	1 tbsp

For the stir-frying:

Vegetable oil	3 tbsp
Ginger (*adrak*), chopped	2 tsp
Garlic (*lasan*) cloves, chopped	4
Tofu, cubed	450 gm
Onions, thinly sliced	2 cups
Broccoli	450 gm
Cashew nuts (*kaju*)	1 cup
Soya sauce	3 tbsp

Method:

1. **For the sauce,** whisk together the peanut or almond butter with hot water into a uniform mixture in a small bowl. Add the remaining ingredients; mix and keep aside.

2. **For the stir-frying,** heat 1 tbsp oil in a pan; stir-fry half the ginger and half the garlic. Add the tofu cubes and stir-fry again. Mix this with the sauce.
3. Heat the remaining oil in another pan; sauté the remaining ginger and garlic. Add the onions and sauté for another 6-8 minutes. Add the broccoli, cashew nuts, and soya sauce. Keep the broccoli deep green throughout the process of sautéing. Toss the mixture with the sauce and serve with steamed rice.

South-Indian Style Broccoli

Preparation and Cooking time: 30 min. Serves: 4-5

Ingredients:

Broccoli, washed, chopped into 1″ cubes	1 bunch
Vegetable oil	1 tbsp
Cumin (*jeera*) seeds	1/2 tsp
Black mustard seeds (*rai*)	1/2 tsp
Onion, chopped	1 tbsp
Salt	1/2 tsp
Black pepper (*kali mirch*)	1/2 tsp
Black gram (*urad dal*)	1 tsp
Sesame seeds (*til*)	1 tsp
Asafoetida (*hing*)	1/8 tsp

Method:

1. Heat the oil in a pan; add cumin and mustard seeds. When the seeds start to pop, add the remaining ingredients except the broccoli and cook for 1-2 minutes.
2. Now add the broccoli and stir. Cook until bright green and tender.

Lemon Garlic Broccoli

Preparation and Cooking time: 10 min. Serves: 3

Ingredients:

Broccoli, cut into florets	500 gm
Olive oil	3 tbsp
Garlic (*lasan*) cloves, chopped	2
Lemon (*nimbu*) juice	3 tbsp
Salt to taste	

Method:

1. Steam the broccoli in a non-stick pan for about 4-6 minutes or till it is tender but firm.
2. Heat the oil in a non-stick skillet on medium heat; add the garlic and sauté for a minute. Add the cooked broccoli, lemon juice, and salt; stir briefly. Serve hot.

This is a rich source of vitamin A and C. Children will develop a taste for this almost immediately.

Deep-fried Eggplant

Preparation and Cooking time: 15 min. Serves: 4-5

Ingredients:

Eggplant (*baingan*), large	1
Salt and black pepper (*kali mirch*) to taste	
All purpose flour (*maida*)	1/4 cup
Egg	1
Milk or water	2 tbsp
Breadcrumbs (fine)	1/4 cup
Vegetable oil for deep-frying	

Method:

1. Beat the egg with the milk or water. Keep aside.
2. Peel the eggplant (you can leave the skin on if you like) and cut into 1/4"-thick rounds. Sprinkle with salt and pepper, and coat with the flour. Dip the rounds in the egg-milk mixture and coat with breadcrumbs.
3. Heat the oil in a thick-bottomed skillet; deep-fry the eggplant until golden brown. Remove and drain the excess oil on paper towels. Serve immediately.

Great way to introduce your child to eggplant, a rich source of iron. This can be eaten rolled up with a soft hot roti or like a snack.

Spicy Cumin Eggplant

Preparation and Cooking time: 15 min. Serves: 4-5

Ingredients:

Eggplant (*baingan*), medium-sized, peeled	1
Vegetable oil	4 tbsp
Mustard seeds (*rai*)	2 tsp
Cumin (*jeera*) seeds	3/4 tsp
Turmeric (*haldi*) powder	1/2 tsp
Asafoetida (*hing*)	1/8 tsp
Onion, chopped	1 tbsp
Salt	1 tsp
Chickpea flour (*besan*)	1/2 cup
Red chilli powder	1/2 tsp
Coriander (*dhaniya*) powder	2 tsp

Method:

1. Cut the eggplant into 1″ cubes.
2. Heat the oil in a pan; add mustard and cumin seeds. When the seeds begin to pop, add turmeric powder, asafoetida, and onion.
3. Add the eggplant and salt; mix well. Cook covered, for about 5 minutes, on medium heat or till the eggplant turns soft. Remove the lid and add chickpea flour and the remaining ingredients. Mix well and cook for another 5-7 minutes, uncovered, on medium heat. Make sure that the flour does not stick. Remove and serve with rice or roti.

Ginger Garlic Asparagus

Preparation and Cooking time: 10 min. Serves: 4

Ingredients:

Asparagus	450 gm
Salad oil	2 tbsp
Garlic (*lasan*) clove, large, minced or pressed	1
Ginger (*adrak*), fresh, grated	1/2-1 tsp
Water	2 tbsp

Method:

1. Snap off and throw away the tough ends of the asparagus, then cut them into spears approximately 1/4"-slanting slices.
2. Heat the oil on high heat in a wok or a heavy skillet; add garlic and ginger and stir quickly. Add asparagus and stir-fry for 1 minute. Add the water; cover and cook the asparagus until tender but crisp to bite, this would take around 2-3 minutes.
3. Serve hot.

Steamed Asparagus

Preparation and Cooking time: 10 min. Serves: 3-4

Ingredients:

Asparagus, washed, trimmed	450 gm
Water	1 cup
Vegetable oil	1 tbsp

Method:

1. Boil the water in a heavy medium-sized skillet. Add the asparagus and cover the skillet. Steam till it is tender.
2. Drain and add vegetable oil and serve.

Instead of vegetable oil you could use olive oil with a crushed garlic added to the top before serving.

Spiced Mushrooms in Yoghurt

Preparation and Cooking time: 15-20 min. Serves: 3-4

Ingredients:

Mushrooms (*gucchi*), washed, dried, sliced	1 1/2 cups
Vegetable oil	2 tbsp
Cumin (*jeera*) seeds	1/2 tsp
Yoghurt (*dahi*)	1 cup
Cumin powder	1/2 tsp
Salt	1/4 tsp

Method:

1. Heat the oil in a saucepan; add cumin seeds and mushrooms. When the seeds turn brown, reduce heat and cook for 5-7 minutes. Remove and keep aside to cool.
2. Add the yoghurt and mix in the remaining ingredients; serve with steamed brown rice.

Tofu and Mushrooms

Preparation and Cooking time: 15 min. Serves: 3-4

Ingredients:

Tofu	450 gm
Dried mushrooms	6
Water	2 cups
Soya sauce	1 tbsp
Black pepper (*kali mirch*)	1/4 tsp

Method:

1. Soak the mushrooms in water for 20 minutes. Drain. Cut the tofu into 1" cubes.
2. Cook the mushrooms and tofu in a large pan on medium heat for 1/2 an hour. When done, add soya sauce and black pepper; mix well. Serve.

Tastes great with plain rice or as a snack or side dish. The dish helps in strengthening the immune system and improves concentration.

Gujarati Dal

Preparation and Cooking time: 40 min. Serves: 6-8

Ingredients:

Split green gram (*moong dal*), soaked for 2 hours, drained	1 3/4 cups
Vegetable oil	1 tbsp
Mustard seeds (*rai*)	1/2 tsp
Turmeric (*haldi*) powder	1/2 tsp
Asafoetida (*hing*)	1/8 tsp
Water	6 1/2 cups
Green pepper (*Shimla mirch*), chopped (optional)	1/4 tsp
Barley malt or brown rice syrup	1 1/2 tsp
Lemon (*nimbu*) juice	1 1/2 tsp
Coriander (*dhaniya*) powder	1 tsp
Garlic (*lasan*) clove	1
Cinnamon (*dalchini*)	1/2 tsp
Curry powder	1/4 tsp
Salt	1 tsp

Method:

1. Heat the oil in a large pan; add the mustard seeds. When the seeds start spluttering, add turmeric powder, asafoetida, green gram, water, and the remaining ingredients. Mix this well.
2. Cover the pan and cook for 30 minutes or till soft.
3. Serve garnished with green coriander and accompanied with either roti or rice.

Simple Vegetable Curry

Preparation and Cooking time: 40 min. Serves: 9-10

Ingredients:

Green peas (*hara muttar*), fresh or frozen peas	1 cup
Carrots (*gajar*), chopped	1 cup
Potatoes, chopped	1 cup
Beans or asparagus, chopped	2 cups
Vegetable oil	2 tbsp
Cumin (*jeera*) seeds	2 tsp
Black mustard seeds (*rai*)	2 tsp
Turmeric (*haldi*) powder	2 tsp
Water	1 1/2 cups
Yoghurt (*dahi*)	1/2 cup
Coriander (*dhaniya*) powder	1 tsp
Salt	1 tsp

Method:

1. Heat the oil in a skillet; add cumin and mustard seeds. When they begin to pop, add turmeric powder and stir for a few seconds. Add the vegetables and water and cook for 15-20 minutes or till tender.
2. Add yoghurt, coriander powder, and salt; mix well. Reduce heat and simmer, uncovered, for another 15-20 minutes.

Spinach and Potato Curry

Preparation and Cooking time: 30 min. Serves: 4-5

Ingredients:

Potatoes, medium-sized	3
Spinach (*palak*)	575 gm
Vegetable oil	1 1/2 tbsp
Mustard seeds (*rai*)	1/2 tsp
Asafoetida (*hing*)	1/8 tsp
Turmeric (*haldi*) powder	1/2 tsp
Water	2 cups
Garlic (*lasan*) cloves, chopped	2
Coriander (*dhaniya*) powder	2 tsp
Lemon (*nimbu*) juice	2 tsp
Green chilli, chopped (optional)	1/2
Salt	1 tsp

Method:

1. Wash the spinach thoroughly in running water. Chop into fine shreds.
2. Cut the potatoes into 1/2" cubes.
3. Heat the oil in a saucepan; add mustard seeds and asafoetida. When the seeds begin to pop, add turmeric powder, potatoes, and water.
4. Cover and simmer on medium heat for 5-7 minutes.

5. Add the spinach, garlic, coriander powder, lemon juice, green chilli, and salt; mix well. Cook covered for an additional 10-15 minutes. Remove and serve hot..

Spicy Hash Brown Potato

Preparation and Cooking time: 45 min. Serves: 10

Ingredients:

Potatoes, medium-sized	5
Sour cream	1 cup
Celery soup, undiluted	1/2 cup
Mozzarella cheese, grated	200 gm
Salt	1 1/2 tsp
Dried basil	1/2 tsp
Onion, chopped	1
Garlic (*lasan*) clove, minced	1-2
Butter, melted	40 gm
Dried oregano	1 tsp
Red chilli flakes	1-2 tsp

Method:

1. Boil the potatoes. Remove the skin and place in a bowl of cool water.
2. In another bowl, mix the sour cream, celery soup, cheese, salt, basil, and garlic for 1-2 minutes.
3. Mash the boiled potatoes. Mix in the onion and transfer the mixture into a greased 6″ x 10″ baking dish. Pour the cream mixture over the potatoes.
4. Drizzle melted butter over the mixture. Bake at 180°C / 350°F for 45 minutes. Remove and garnish with oregano and red chilli flakes.
5. Serve with warm garlic bread and green salad.

Sweet Chickpeas

Preparation and Cooking time: 20 min. Serves: 4

Ingredients:

Chickpeas (*kabuli chana*), boiled	2 cups
Vegetable oil	1-2 tbsp
Carom seeds (*ajwain*)	1/2 tsp
Asafoetida (*hing*)	1/8 tsp
Parsnips, grated	2 cups
Turmeric (*haldi*) powder	1/2 tsp
Onion, large, chopped	1
Salt	1/2 tsp
Water	1/2 cup
Green coriander (*hara dhaniya*), chopped for garnishing	

Method:

1. Heat the oil in a large pan; add carom seeds and asafoetida, stir till lightly brown.
2. Add the chickpeas, parsnips, turmeric powder, and onion; sauté for around 6 minutes.
3. Add the remaining ingredients and cook for another 10 minutes more or until the parsnip and onions are soft and tender.
4. Serve garnished with green coriander and accompanied with roti or steamed rice.

Oat Bran

Preparation and Cooking time: 40 min. Serves: 6-8

Ingredients:

Oat bran	$1\frac{1}{2}$ cups
Egg, beaten	1
Maple syrup	1 tbsp
Soya milk	2 cups
Vegetable oil	1 tbsp
Baking powder	2 tsp
Salt	1 tsp
Cornmeal	$\frac{3}{4}$ cup
Sunflower seeds	$\frac{1}{4}$ cup

Method:

1. Preheat the oven at 180°C / 350°F.
2. Mix the egg, maple syrup, soya milk, and oil in a bowl.
3. Mix the baking powder, salt, oat bran, cornmeal, and sunflower seeds in another bowl.
4. Mix the contents of both the bowls together into a soupy consistency. Pour this mixture into a greased 8"-baking dish and bake for 20-25 minutes.

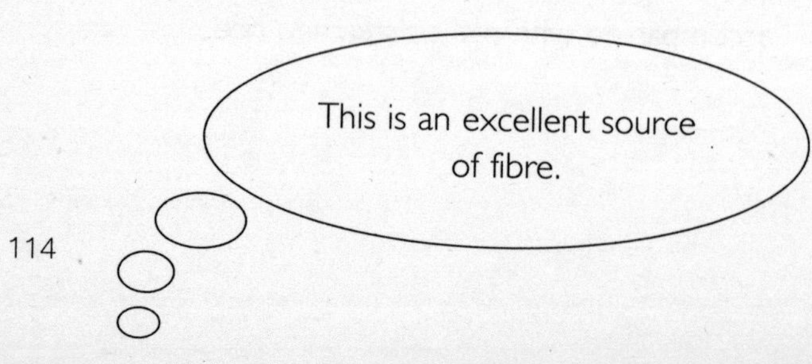

Papaya Salad

Preparation time: 5-10 min. Serves: 2

Ingredients:

Papaya (*papita*), ripe	1
Lemon (*nimbu*) juice	1 tbsp
Salt to taste	

Method:

Wash and slice the papaya into 1/2" cubes. Add salt and lemon juice and mix thoroughly.

This should be eaten on an empty stomach as it clears the extra mucous from the gastrointestinal tract as well as stimulates digestion of protein in the body. The papaya seeds can be eaten with the lemon juice for expulsion of roundworms.

Spiced Yoghurt

Preparation time: 5 min. Makes: 1 cup

Ingredients:

Yoghurt (*dahi*)	1 1/2 cups
Blackstrap molasses	1-2 tsp
Vanilla extract	1/4 tsp

Method:

Stir all the ingredients together and serve.

A mineral and vitamin-rich side dish which helps to calm the nerves. It is rich in iron, calcium, sulphur, and vitamin B.

Sweets and Desserts

Muesli Bars

Preparation and Cooking time: 30 min. Makes: 20

Ingredients:

Unsalted butter	1/2 cup
Brown sugar	1/3 cup
Honey	3 tbsp
Quick cooking oats	1 cup
Hazelnuts, chopped	1/3 cup
Coconut (*nariyal*), shredded	1/3 cup
Sesame (*til*) seeds	1/3 cup

Method:

1. Preheat the oven at 180°C / 350°F.
2. Grease and flour an 11" x 7" baking dish and keep aside.
3. Combine butter, brown sugar, and honey together in a pan and cook, stirring continuously, on low heat. When the butter melts and the sugar dissolves remove from heat.
4. Mix in the oats, hazelnuts, coconut, and sesame seeds. Stir until well blended.
5. Press this mixture evenly into the prepared baking dish and bake for 15-18 minutes or till the top is golden brown. Remove and keep aside to cool.

6. Cut them into even bars and store in airtight dry jars for a couple of days.

This makes a great lunch box treat and after-school snack for kids. Preferably eaten in winter, as they stay fresh for a longer time and provides energy during the day.

Chocolate Cornflake Balls

Preparation and Cooking time: 10 min. Makes: 12

Ingredients:

Plain chocolate bars	4
Cornflakes, crushed	3-4 cups

Method:

1. Melt the chocolate bars in a bowl over boiling water, and stir continuously till it melts.
2. Add the cornflakes and mix them together. Keep aside to cool.
3. Divide the mixture equally into small portions and shape into balls. Refrigerate until they harden up.

Kids could also join in the preparation. This can be stored in an airtight jar for up to 3 days.

Jaggery Wheat Flour Rolls

Preparation and Cooking time: 20-30 min. Makes: 10

Ingredients:

Jaggery (*gur*)	250 gm
Water	1 cup
Wheat flour (*atta*)	250 gm
Aniseed (*saunf*)	1 tsp
Salt	1/2 tsp
Dried coconut (*nariyal*), finely chopped	1/2
Vegetable oil for frying the rotis	

Method:

1. In a heavy-bottomed pan, melt the jaggery in water stirring continuously till the mixture is of dropping consistency. Remove and keep aside to cool.
2. In a flat pan, knead the flour with the cooled and melted jaggery. Add aniseed, salt, and dried coconut; mix thoroughly.
3. Divide the dough into 10 equal portions and roll out into thick rotis.
4. Heat a skillet and lay a roti flat on it. Cook on low heat adding 1 tsp oil along the sides while cooking. Flip and cook the other side till golden brown. Remove and repeat till all are done.
5. Serve hot.

The rotis can be kept in an airtight jar and eaten over a period of 3-4 days. It is especially good for the winter months as it helps keep the body warm, providing your child with a lot of energy.

Fried Bananas

Preparation and Cooking time: 10-15 min. Serves: 2-4

Ingredients:

Bananas (*kela*), large	3
Rice powder	5 tbsp
Water	1/2 cup
Salt	1/4 tsp
Cumin (*jeera*) seeds	1/2 tsp
Vegetable oil	4 tbsp

Method:

1. Peel and slice the bananas lengthwise and refrigerate for 10 minutes.
2. In a large bowl, mix the rice powder with water, salt, and cumin seeds and make a smooth batter.
3. Heat the oil in a frying pan on medium heat. Coat the bananas with the batter till completely covered and fry till golden brown. Repeat till all are fried.

This should be eaten hot,
as soon as it is ready.

Mixed Up Cake

Preparation and Cooking time: 1 hr. Serves: 2-4

Ingredients:

All purpose flour (*maida*)	3 cups
Baking powder	2 tsp
Salt	1 tsp
White sugar, crushed	2 cups
Cocoa	1/2 cup
White vinegar (*sirka*)	2 tsp
Vegetable oil	3/4 cup
Vanilla essence	1 tsp
Water (room temperature)	2 cups

Method:

1. Preheat the oven to 180°C / 350°F. Take a 9" x 9" baking pan and mix all the dry ingredients together until lump free.
2. Take a large spoon and make 3 holes in this mixture. Pour the vinegar, oil, and vanilla essence in the three holes.
3. Pour the water over the entire mixture and mix thoroughly. Bake for 40-45 minutes.

Banana on a Stick

Preparation time: 1 hr. Serves: 2-4

Ingredients:

Banana (*kela*), large, ripe	1/2
Wooden thin sticks	2-4

Additional choices:

Honey, wheat germ, shredded coconut

Method:

1. Peel and cut the banana lengthwise into two. Fix the wooden sticks into the banana slices.
2. Wrap the slices in a plastic wrap and freeze them for around 45 minutes.
3. When frozen remove the wrapper and dip the sticks into honey or shredded coconut or wheat germ.

Alternatively, if you are feeling creative try dipping the banana sticks into melted chocolate.

Glossary of Food and Cooking Terms

Batter: A mixture of flour, liquid and sometimes other ingredients of a thin, creamy consistency.

Blend: To mix together thoroughly two or more ingredients.

Coat: To cover food that is to be fried with flour, egg and breadcrumbs or batter.

Dough: A thick mixture of uncooked flour and liquid, often combined with other ingredients: the mixture can be handled as a solid mass.

Fry: To cook in hot fat or oil. In the case of shallow frying only a small quantity of fat is used in a shallow pan. The food must be turned halfway through to cook both sides. In the case of deep-frying, sufficient fat is used to cover the food completely.

Garnish: An edible decoration added to a savoury or sweet dish to improve its appearance.

Grease: To coat the surface of a dish or tin with fat to prevent food from sticking to it.

Grind: To reduce hard food such as pulses, lentils, rice, and so forth, to fine or coarse paste in a grinder or blender.

Knead: To work a dough by hand or machine until smooth.

Marinade: A seasoned mixture of oil, vinegar, lemon juice, and so forth, in which meat, poultry or fish is left for some time to soften and add flavour to it.

Patty: A small individual pie.

Purée: To press food through a fine sieve or blend it in a blender or food processor to a smooth, thick mixture.

Rub in: To incorporate the fat into flour using the fingertips.

Sauté: To cook in an open pan in hot, shallow fat, tossing the food to prevent it from sticking.

Seasoning: Salt, pepper, spices, herbs, and so forth, added to give depth of flavour.

Sift: To shake a dry ingredient through a sieve or flour sifter, to remove lumps.

Simmer: To boil gently on low heat.

Steam: To cook food in steam. Generally food to be steamed is put in a perforated container which is placed above a pan of boiling water. The food should not come into contact with the water.

Stir: To mix with a circular action, usually with a spoon, fork, or spatula.

Index

DRINKS AND BEVERAGES
Almond Milk 50
Banana Orange Smoothie . . .51
Blended Sunrise 52
Juicy Date Shake 53
Hot Ginger Tea 54
Hot Nutmeg Milk 55
Iron-rich Breakfast Drink 56
Maple Syrup Shake 57
Pistachio Milk 58
Honeyed Milk 59
Soothing Milk 60
Wake Up Shake 62

SNACKS AND STARTERS
Banana Bread 64
Banana Hot Dogs 65
Brown Bread Sandwich 66
Cheese Deluxe 67
Corn 'n' Peanut Balls 90
Cream Cheese Roll ups 68
Edible Face 69
Egg Spread 75
Egg Salad 76
Eggless Egg Salad 77
Eggplant Rice Patties 83
Flip Flop Egg 78
Fresh Coriander Chutney . . .92
Fried Tomatoes 'n' Eggs 79
French Fried Tomatoes 70
Green Potato Patties 84
Sliced Eggplant 71
Hasty Tasty Haystacks 73
Mostly Toasted 72
Mushroom and Peas 86
Olive Cheese Melts 81
Potato Cheese Balls 74
Quick Pancakes 82
Salted Cashews 89
Sesame Spinach 91
Steamed Eggs 80
Steamed Sweet Beetroots . . .87
Sweet Figs and Prunes 88

MAIN COURSE
Artichokes 94
Bean Burritos 95
Cajun Red Beans 97
Deep-fried Eggplant 102
Ginger Garlic Asparagus . . .104
Gujarati Dal 108
Lemon Garlic Broccoli 101
Oat Bran 114
Papaya Salad 115
Simple Vegetable Curry 109
South-Indian Style Broccoli .100
Spicy Cumin Eggplant 103
Spiced Mushrooms
in Yoghurt 106
Spiced Yoghurt 116
Spicy Hash Brown Potato . .112
Spinach and Potato Curry . .110
Steamed Asparagus 105
Stir-Fried Broccoli and Tofu . .98
Sweet Chickpeas 113
Tofu and Mushrooms 107

SWEETS AND DESSERTS
Banana on a Stick 125
Chocolate Cornflake Balls . .120
Fried Bananas 123
Jaggery Wheat Flour Rolls . .121
Mixed Up Cake 124
Muesli Bars 118
Sweet Potato Pudding 122